CURES

Jo Brandon was born in Essex in 1986 and is now based in West Yorkshire. Her working life has been varied, including roles as a domestic for the Royal Household, a tour guide, Creative Writing Coordinator for the Koestler Trust and an administrator for the Poetry Society and Poetry School.

Jo graduated with a degree in Creative Writing from Bretton Hall, University of Leeds in 2007. She now works as a freelance poetry editor, librettist and literary events host. In 2018 she was Bradford Literature Festival's first Digital Poet in Residence. Her poetry is widely published in magazines and anthologies including *The North*, *Poetry Review*, *Butcher's Dog*, *Magma*, *Popshot* and *Brittle Star*.

Jo's debut pamphlet, *Phobia*, was published in 2012 and her first full-length collection, *The Learned Goose*, was published in 2015, both with Valley Press.

# Cures

## Jo Brandon

*Valley Press*

First published in 2021 by Valley Press
Woodend, The Crescent, Scarborough, YO11 2PW
www.valleypressuk.com

ISBN 978-1-912436-55-2
Cat. no. VP0176

A CIP record for this book is available from the British Library.

Cover and text design by Peter Barnfather.
Cover painting (*The Physician*) by Gerard Dou
[courtesy Rijksmuseum, Netherlands].
Edited by Jamie McGarry.

Printed and bound in Great Britain by
Imprint Digital, Upton Pyne, Exeter.

# Contents

BED FELLOWS: HYSTERIA & MELANCHOLIA

Sowing  13
Staying Under  14
Visiting Mary Toft  15
Wednesday's child  16
Widow Raleigh  18
Bonesetter  19
Muse, or that other thing…  20
Crow Hill Bog Burst  23
We are volcanoes  24
Three Ages  25
Kneading  28
That dress  29
Shift  30
Candied  31
Lilliput Lane  33
Bonnie with Angel  35

GRANDE EROTISME & BOTTLED ECSTASY

Venus and Mercury  39
Walter's Wife  40
Miss An-nym—s, C-m S—n Lane, London.  42
Heart stopping  43
Seeking true ideograph  44
No festival more glorious  45
Drunkard's Cloak  46
Prescription  47
Power Sale  48
*Bon Appétit* and breathe  50
In search of Heathcliff…  51

MALADY-RIDDLED

I Was Mr Hoare's Pig-man, 1817  55
The Strangle-hold  57
High Society, 1844  59
Cataracts  60
Mary's creature  61
Waste: A History  62
In Stereo  64
Town Hall Steps, Leeds  65
Octopus Dreams  66
Salt-song  67

SETTLE & SOOTHE

Pontefract Cake  71
Bentley & Tempest Ltd.  72
Headingley's Zoological Gardens  73
How to be a Hermit:  75
Second Date  76
New house  77
Those hours  78
Week 10  79
Once a year  80
Reverse  81

Notes on the poems  83
Acknowledgements  91

For God's sake build not your faith upon Tradition,
'tis as rotten as a rotten Post.

– Nicholas Culpeper, *The English Physician*


Selfishness must always be forgiven you know,
because there is no hope of a cure.

– Jane Austen, *Mansfield Park*

# PART ONE

# Bed fellows:
# Hysteria
# & Melancholia

# Sowing

It is usual for polite ladies to start a florilegium,
to imitate the Bear's Eyes and Tulips
sketched by Merian and Marshal,
to sit serenely in the sun, fans fluttering petals
from their still-life aspirations.

It is not unheard of for them to learn the names
of the intimate parts of flowers,
to teeter on the fringes of idolatry,
develop a mania for new-found forms of beauty:
nature's prerogative in bloom.

But I do think it unhealthy
that she recumbs in the heat,
freckling like a ripe dairymaid.
That she lay, hair unbound, on the lawn –
basking as though Zeus had turned himself
to grass and daisies.

I believe it must be unnatural for her
to steal out in the moonlight
and plant parsley in our window-box,
for her to whisper sweet words to it,
as though to a child – I believe
she has been poisoned by the moon,
forgotten that the night is dark
and should be still.

There is a fashion now
for the *Hortus Conclusus*;
gardens walled.
She believes I take this too literally.
It is time, I said, to remember
the pleasures of the home.

# Staying Under

My mother was turned away
from her neighbour's door, with me
in arms, though she were lonely enough
to eat her own hair,
but what is loneliness
next to the transgression of ill-wishing,
the ill-wishing a woman brings if
she leaves her bed too soon,
goes from under her husband's roof,
knocks on any other than the church door,
is unclean, does pollute with newborn cries
and the smell of unchanged sheets.

I will never be turned away, like her.
Nine months, I've spent, gathering reeds,
loosening limp heather, pulling at straws,
weaving a smaller roof, my husband's in miniature,
that will perch over my hair like a Spanish hood –
a daintier thatch that will protect their luck.
A twist and turn about the proper way of things
I'm sure, they'll say. They'd prefer to bind me abed
with close walls and the stifling heat of summer-lit fires,
but they can't chastise the rightness out of this.

I could almost have laughed to Mother Moon
these past nights, as I stole big-bellied up our ladder,
swifter than the fox that eyes my coop, sure-footed,
I thin my husband's roof while, stonily, he sleeps.
Now, I have my churching veil, my saint's gable –
a talisman of patched logic, I will not step foot
from under-roof too soon.

# Visiting Mary Toft

You should have gone out of town for the rabbits,
but that's not really what I came to say.
I think the story is muddled in people's minds;
you are a hoaxster, a fraud, a beguiler of clever men –
these are facts, fair enough, but you are also a woman brimful
of tears, a woman that once lost a baby, a baby that,
for whatever God's purpose, did look more rabbit than son,
you felt his movements change; the coarse contractions
of old magic. They say a hare crossed your path,
and that's when all your troubles started. You sought to expel
all long-eared curses in advance of the next one, the bonny one.
Your womb was open to suggestion and all your impish fears
did set up a maypole there and dance around your hopes
and sadness. So inserting a furry hind leg, an eel's tail, a cat's paw
seemed no mistruth compared to what you'd already seen,
you were not ready to be emptied yet, and they would not see
what they were not eager to see – I believe you
would have healed and closed up that portal to bad luck
soon enough, had others with no excuse
not jumped on your back, but there we are,
sometimes misfortune is like money – it begets itself
with no scruple, and since you could make no sense of why
you did what you did, they helped themselves – stretched
your tall tale.

# Wednesday's child

Though bedsore and leech-humoured, I took advice,
coin-hewn, from a hunched, mumping beldam.
She ran yellow nails over his pale flesh, laughed
when I said he was caul-born, gave me waxy ointments,
instructed that I lay his father's coat over him, tie string
on his crib – end to end, sprinkle holy water on the boards,
shoulder-toss salt over the threshold, put a shoe in the rafters,
etch dog Latin on the sill, pillow-stuff my prayers

> *sleep, sleep, sleep,*
> *your baby will grow*
> *whether you know him or not,*
> *sleep, sleep, sleep,*
> *woe will make your heart slow,*
> *if we cast him back now he'd only rot*
> *weep your eyes dry and*
> *sleep, sleep, sleep*

They say his teeth came too soon, I chose the wrong man
to temper him, his name was poor-given, I boasted too much
of his fairness, new clothes are ill-wishes, my milk was tainted,
he supped on sour dreams in my belly.
They say I saw them come and held open the door.
They say,

> *sleep, sleep, sleep,*
> *your baby will grow*
> *whether you know him or not,*
> *sleep, sleep, sleep,*
> *woe will make your heart slow,*
> *if we cast him back now he'd only rot,*
> *weep your eyes dry and*
> *sleep, sleep, sleep*

riddle-tongued and cruel, my boy is now a shadow
to the baby in the crib, they say I will feel his fingers
graze my cheek while I sleep

*sleep, sleep, sleep*

# Widow Raleigh

*after Elizabeth Throckmorton, wife of Sir Walter Raleigh*

She winds the silk cords around her fingers
in a way she can't recall winding his hair
but memories are meant to be revised,
like histories; death clears
the mind – *a sharp medicine,*
leaving the best of the deceased behind.
She meditates on this in her closet,
the Saints painted on the walls
rub a soothing salve into her heart, as her hands,
partnered in prayer, form a roof over his head,
hearthed between her knees in a velvet bag:
red and gold, the colours
that became him most, tailored close-fit
to carry his preserved crown.
She finds comfort in its heaviness,
the way it bumps her thigh when she walks,
like a dog having retrieved a grouse,
how her posture has tilted, lopsided
as his sweet morning smile,
which was not preserved;
there is not much to be done
once rigor and rictus set to.

# Bonesetter

*A largely, though not entirely,
made up account of Sally Mapp, 1737.*

You've been asked so often that you say,
with tongue-filled cheek, *I feel it in my marrow.*
You don't,
you feel it in your hands: sensitive, skilled, strong,
but you have a bosom that recalls their pap-ladling nurses
and you smile while you talk, so it can't be knowledge,
nor do you have a blacksmith's arms; uncanny, that's all –
they've all seen the occasional calf with two heads.
They'll watch you work but you can't smoke your cigars
at their club, they'll censure you with matronly tuts if you curse
and though *Lord Sir Mr* will beg a favour of you to set
a money-crippled spine, you'll never get a place at St George's –
not even Bedlam is hiring, *you expect us to believe you learnt
from your father, what cock and ball,*

*Bull?*

*No dear, really, where are your cock and balls?*
They don't listen when you compare feeling for breaks
to running your hands over woodgrain, don't look
into the eyes of one table-fixed with pain and wait
for great intakes of breath to pop joints back again
they listen to their own quickened hearts, jingle of coin,
thickness of cards being left in the hall.
You met one who didn't like direct contact with skin,
another closed his eyes while his saw was wrist-deep in thigh –
the anatomists were gleeful that day, one wanted
to take you to bed but you saw him spit gristle at dinner,
*Oh Cracked Sally, you're the only one that can set my bone.*
Fool-you, fellow you took fancy to had his dead wife
pickled at home – a drinks rest fixed to her glass-fronted case.
You wouldn't let a single one near you if you needed fixing,
you joke, too often – and in company, that
you'd rather a sapient pig took up scalpel and bistoury
than any of those *learned men.*

# Muse, or that other thing...

I

*Bathing at Gower Street*

Once your ears are submerged you enter a different world. It's easy to look far away when you are. He says *you are a palette of tumbled peaches and sun-bleached poppies.* I watch my fixed curls dissolve into waves; into foam. Though warm water undoes the knots of living, I keep my limbs stiff; he thinks beauty is most beautiful when it is still (*animation is not for the immortal*) but my mind wonders and if I am quick I can flick an unseen toe to ripple cooling waters. Beneath me the lamps work as hard as they can to keep the chill afternoon from this tub: I people the space beneath me, between clawed brass feet, with a brigade of elfin men making bellows of themselves for my sake, blowing their warm little lungs out or stoking fires the size of finger-nails, splinters for kindling. We keep the light but it toys with him, it keeps me frozen; there are many things not their true selves till the sun is set. He has taken as much of me as he needs into the paint, but every living thing must have a shadow. Rivers run deep on my finger-tips, down silt-patterned skin, fields are furrowed on my toes, a flea circus could retire from the metropolis and live off the land on my water-ploughed torso. My hair, like mother's tea leaves, begin to form unexpected things: violets tightly tangled amongst a bed of weeds, vase-cut flowers drooping, briars gathered about me. Above the water my face has no feeling, beneath it my arms and legs are twice as thick as they were before but I could sink further still, down into another, other, world. I could make an uncanny disappearance, no wet foot-prints, just a void of darkened hair.

## II

*Emily's Book*

I imagine she had her reasons. I imagine they sounded plausible at the
time, necessary even, but wasn't there something that shrivelled and
blackened within her along with those pages? Did she wish she
hadn't? Even while the smoke made her cough, did she try and pluck
it out but, reflexes dulled by grief, found it too far gone to save? Did
she read it? Read it often enough to write it out again? Is it etched line
by line around the house in all the places Emily ran her hands: the
banister, lip of the ottoman, backs of chairs, door frames, glass panes,
her hobnail boots, or did she want to smother it in a shawl of myth?
Did she fling it upwards towards a home-lit bonfire, watch the pages
catch the air like collared doves, did she stride into the house and wait
till the ashes were gone, having swept away any strange and sombre
powers incanted by those words, or did she think she was beckoning,
goading, holding her back by the hem? Did she think the End needed
re-writing?

III

*Julian of Norwich*

I imagine her alone, back stooped, neck stiff, shoulders fixed in a posture suited to devotion, her mouth mumbling the words as she writes – as they tumble too fast from above to have formed in any fallible, bodily way. My image of her blurs the closer I get to her hands – the mechanics, the labour of her writing is so different to the clean, tapping fluidity I take for granted. I imagine ink staining the inside of her longest finger, smudged on the side of her palm, a smear on her chin, I see round drops of ink fall in thick clots before bleeding thinly into the page, she thinks *how like herring scales or rain from the eaves* and these, in turn, make her think of Christ's perfect blood – it makes me think of the nib scratching on paper and how it sounds like hazelnuts cracking. She must have strengthened the muscles in her hands, writing as she did, even as her eyes weakened in the dim light. I imagine her flexing her hands before she brings them together to praise Him, meeting one another neatly, like the pages of a closed book.

# Crow Hill Bog Burst

*after Emily Brontë*

Servants may gossip,
inn-fixed men may stew,
households may quarrel
and old friends break faith,
but there is no drama
more heightened
than the will of the moor;
the day that the earth
shook us all loose
and out of the eruption
of mud and water –
soaked, porch-huddled,
struck thunder-deaf
and peat-clod hobbled,
I felt words hard-shaken shift
into my fingertips, felt
stories gush full-silt
into my mouth, as if I too
were a torrent of water
breaking into a flood
and there could be no
damming it now.

# We are volcanoes

*after Ursula K. Le Guin*

There may be quiet years,
years when it seems
they are mountains again,
and mountains bring awe
in their way but you get used
to seeing them in one frame,
expect them always to be
the same fertile ground
for foot-worn paths,
loose-soiled slopes
that need mapping.

There may be quiet years,
when the hardened crust
is cool to the touch and
it seems you could dig
and find only rock and ash –
and maybe the fossils
of more dangerous things.

There may be quiet years
when the plates shift a little,
and the mountain shakes –
some smoke, some heat
but life carries on the same,
no urgency –

> do people not know what it means
> when a mountain moves?

> There may be quiet years
> but this is not one of them

# Three Ages

*after Three Ages of Woman by Gustav Klimt, 1905*

I

My mother teaches me
how to fold and scent my linen,
it is all I can do to stay awake
but I cannot lay down until
corners are tucked and straight.
'You can do a lot of things half-well
but bed-making is not one of them.'
I do not see the necessity of crisp,
unstained sheets when they will only
tangle around my cry-startled limbs;
she says it will matter to me one day,
to have a sanctuary, a place to love sleep
more and more – 'the old ways have a knack
of preserving themselves – though you, my girl,
will fray'.

## II

Cheeks round as ripe plums,
filled with mouth-blessed,
milk-wet hands that wander
and tangle in heat-scented hair.
I will unknot her fingers
when sleep relaxes incubated need,
will indulge my day-dreams,
vivid as stories caught
in colour-touched glass,
of her many, many years
as soon as her breathing
steadies,

          her breath
fills all the consciousness
I have to spare
for the hard-as-stones place
we gradually inhabit,
but we are not there yet,
she brought my waters
out with her and there
we bob – in and out of now,
in and out of when,
in and out

          in and out.

## III

Born shrunken-limbed but plump –
when young I floated in the water, now,
like a gnawed bone I'm sinking to the bottom
where my colour is exhaled as tiny bubbles:
these slow years. Nobody fishes to retrieve me.
My Grandmother said, 'No use dropping the bucket
down an emptied well'. At least I'm not dunked down
the village well or bricked up in the chimney breast,
there is some faint shine to being beside notice,
after all, it is always the old woman that's a hex –
or the unmarried girl, the latter of which
is fair – fairer – she still has her duty to do,
dues to pay with winning smiles and compliance
but the crone has served her time
as obedient child, faithful helpmeet, kind mother.
Yet age renders her ugly, as if readying to feed the earth
at nature's speed is more uncanny than falling asleep
in the fullness of youth; the fallacy that fruit sours
before it rots – I have always found it sweetest
as it drops.

# Kneading

*Love doesn't just sit there, like a stone;*
*it has to be made, like bread...*
– from *The Lathe of Heaven* by Ursula K. Le Guin

My bread keeps turning out like stones;
loaves leavened like lava – the soft innards
spilling upwards, hardening into crusts,
layers and layers of crust, crumbs
turn to tuff on my tongue.
Start again, knock it back,
hands caked in clastic dough.

Simple recipe that always rose
predictably, now burns itself
into unkind alchemy.
Tooth-broken, sore-knuckled,
I no longer know what to do
with my hands.

# That dress

I remember that dress.
Pink floral on black,
slightly flared silhouette,
button-down
crinkly crepe that Mum always
ironed by mistake.
It would now hang inconspicuously
on the '90s rail at a vintage boutique
but then it was my Victorian dress,
Victorian because it had tie-ribbons at the back;
my entire understanding of corsetry.
I stood in front of the mirror, tying it
tighter and tighter, watching my waist get smaller,
letting the buttons gape, pushing past discomfort,
past hurt, till I heard stitches pull;
the warning gasp fabric gives
right before a tear.
I always stopped there, to protect the seams;
after all, that dress had its limits.

# Shift

*In response to Shakespeare's Sonnet 77.*

It is only 7 hours and 7 minutes until
I can go home.
Sticking a scrap of paper over the lower,
right-hand corner of my screen hasn't helped.
There are still the easy-to-read hands
of the office clock, the twitch of my wrist-watch
and my phone busy with updates –
they have just discovered my computer
gives off UV light, despite this fact I am deficient
in vitamin D from being in here
twenty-eight thousand and eight-hundred seconds a day.
The air conditioning makes my hair brittle,
dries my eyes out and thins my skin;
I have a scholar's stoop from failing to meet
impossible ergonomic standards.
I have created a blank folder on the desktop
where I tap out and save all of my wishes –
they are more or less the same
but listing them feels like invoking a spell.
I will leave them for my successor to find,
I wonder if they'll seem like gibberish to her
or an extension of the list she's left behind.

# Candied

There wasn't a sequence of events,
more a jumble; time bundled up
inside the duvet cover during a spin cycle
and wouldn't shake out.

It started with the little fondant flowers
she made to decorate her cakes
that turned into perfumed mulch
in everyone's mouth but hers;
while outside, in her garden,
all the petioles and stems snapped
under the weight of sugar-paste petals.

It didn't work the other way round;
when she encouraged her clients to eat
the wild daisy-heads decorating the top-tier
they didn't turn into ornate puffs of buttercream.

At the same time her mother started
craving rose lemonade and nowhere
was selling any. Once upon a time
she would have squeezed lemons and roses,
sifted sugar and taken an iced jug to her mother
but now, she didn't dare.

Although icing remained sugary
in her mouth, she imagined the stalky,
wriggly, living counterpart
of all she ate;
everything tasted bewildered.

The stress of it made her sweat at night,
so that when she woke, there was a salty shadow
of herself that never left the bed.
She stopped baking.
It was the responsible thing to do
but it's an ending that has never satisfied
anyone I've ever spoken to.

# Lilliput Lane

She built a village centred around
a Norman church, gravestones
with names etched too small to read.
She kept them behind glass in a cabinet
that came ready-assembled.
She wasn't proscriptive like some philanthropists;
the villagers were welcome to drink, quarrel and hang
their washing out whichever day they pleased.

The village was all up hill and down dale;
shelves of jutting landscape that lent
the uppermost cottages a Top Withens air.
Every house was detached with a threading
beck out back, their gardens linked
by ginnels of varnished wood.

Though it was a sleepy place
the village shop was always open,
sherbet and biscuit stocks never depleted.

Their celestials were wire-hung
painted plates. To any villagers looking up
there really was an old man in the moon
and a cushioned kitten in the sun.
I liked to be the last one to bed,
to switch off the lights and set
an eclipse in motion.

After dusting for pocket money
I let my fingers creep across their gardens
like detached legs or spider crawls,
I felt someone ought to delicately
violate their lawns.

That's why there was something
of the atomic bomb
about seeing them pulled full-fistedly
from the cabinet, mushroom clouds
of newspaper swallowing them
ready for a Sunday car-boot.

Quietly shaken, like the little people inside,
staring at the empty cabinet, sun-bleached
and dappled with kidney-bean shaped blotches,
I longed, despite years of yellow dusters,
to fill it over-again with all the same things.

# Bonnie with Angel

*after Alec Soth's portrait*

Bonnie is loved by the angels.
Sometimes they crowd around her so tightly
she worries her stocking tops will pop
from the squeeze of His almighty love.

Bonnie loves her angels,
especially the one that showed itself,
and was pressed like a dried flower
between the click of her camera's shutter,
to shy off the naysayers who rascal
the Reverend during his TV phone-ins.

The Reverend loves Bonnie's angel.
He, and the rest of the congregation,
sent Bonnie a gilt frame; it protects
Bonnie's angel, gives it weight,
makes it easier to rest that angel in her lap.

Bonnie is sick of being asked if she likes
crystals and incense, it is clear
she likes 'things as is, to be things as seen'
and Bonnie can show you her angel –
you can't un-see Bonnie's angel.

# PART TWO

# Grande Erotisme
# & Bottled Ecstasy

# Venus and Mercury

If the suffumigations, inunctions, steamings,
poultices, clysters, lettings and sweated fevers
don't plug these leaking humours, if the impostume
carbuncles, cankerous ulcers, gumboils, festered furuncles,
pus-pursed abscesses, blistering aphthas and vesicating
sores increase, if the scirrhus hardness refuses
to allay under ointments of calomel and heartsease,
if elixirs of vitriol, Holy Wood and henbane balm are ineffective,
if the foul chancres and papules are inflamed despite prayers,
pilgrimage and the kissing of relics, if the nose is saddled, well,
in short, the Grandgore has already taken last-lease of your bones.

# Walter's Wife

*after Walter's My Secret Life, 1888*

Walter wonders why we went from wedded bliss
to conjugal nothingness.
In all his scrawlings he cannot note the moment
he lost his wife.
I have a good memory though, and at first-thought
I can conjure that afternoon, still our paper year,
he came home stinking
of over-sweet violets and cheap talcum powder,
he was flushed, unable to meet my eye, walking
almost on tip-toes.

I could imagine what had happened behind those
gaudily draped windows I'm not meant to pass,
I am a married woman not a nun. What recourse
did I have? We can have a happy home – or not.

I thought if he scrubs himself clean,
if I can smell our rose water and lavender cologne on him,
if he is shy and hangdog, if he is too sorry and ashamed
to come near me for this while, if he discreetly apologises
with courtly gifts and tokens, if he lets slip a reason why
he might have broken faith,
then all this might be made well, something to forget,
something that never happens again

but he did not seek soap and water,
kept the smell on him
like the club's waft of cigars.
His flush faded quickly
and everything was peaceful in him again
by bedtime.
I was silent and still,
stiff as a corpse, when he put himself on me,
this thing that was just for us –
he still wore her dewy acceptance of him.
I could not even turn into her thin arms
and warm bosom to complain, as he had.
I am no different to her – for him;
one an outdoor privy,
the other a chamber pot.

# Miss An-nym—s, C-m S—n Lane, London.

*A letter to a certain Gentleman via The Times,*
*upon reading Harris's latest List.*

When I buy something, a pie or a dress, say
I want to know what it is exact: butter-crust filled
with meat and gravy, or pink-striped, one darning,
one faded stain. Plain like that. I don't
want to know the cook's life story, who else
eats his pies, nor where he found the meat;
I don't want to know who spoiled the dress
nor how fine it looked in former times, I don't want
a cheap bouquet of flowery language obscuring my view
of things I'll buy any which way –
the pie-man doesn't want to quibble over his filling
nor the rag-lady over the fit and nor do I want to be the Venus
of Clapham, or the soiled Rose of Waterloo, none of us do,
so find us when you want us, there's no use
being coy around that, but say no more, spill no purple ink
and I'll not pass it on down the row about your crooked pen.

# Heart stopping

Oh, my sweet Angina, you choke me up;
how my atrium aches for you,
my chest flutters and I am dropsy in your arms,
you leave me lockjawed, just a glimpse makes my heart burn,
my pyrosis bursts into flame, my dyspepsia keeps me up all night,
like our rambles through Naples and France, my mercurial darling.
Oh, my dear Carditis – you make my heart swell.
When you're gone, heavenly Cardioptosis, my heart sinks;
thoughts of you make my pulse quicken, you turn my lips blue,
my swollen fingers fumble for you as I reach
acute aortic aneurysm.

# Seeking true ideograph

We dared not look inside our chests,
blindly pierced our hearts –
poor–shot Eros riddled them
with consequence,
bound love and heart together
using herbs, sweet words,
shared lore – chose *Silphium* seeds,
shaped like buttocks, to fill
that unknowable echo-cavern
of quickened pulse. In place of valves
and throbbing muscle we chose
a complete and rounded graphic.
Uncomplicated, no in, no out, no
stopping.
An organ set like a gem in a ribcage foil.
It tapers to a sharp point, I grant them that,
and symmetry is beauty – I don't suggest
we send a Valentine of fennel bulbs or ginger roots
or aniseed fruit instead, but I am suspicious of a heart
that looks as though it could break so neatly in two,
that looks as though it would mend and work again.
A broken heart should look like it's been pulled apart;
pure gore, stain everything –
like love.

# No festival more glorious

It looks as though Zeus has slit the throat of an upstart god,
much-trod marble is washed with blood, air is thick with heat
and flies and the tang of sacrifice, we have oxen bones enough
to build another temple. The crowd is so swollen
I wouldn't know the slick of my own sweat from another's,
a fevered crush of bodies that moves as one from game
to game, while old skin becomes parched as stored figs,
flakes off to reveal new, sun-raw hides; we gleam
beneath the Gods, throats sore from prayer
and favourite-cheering – odds be what they are.
The sprints are longer than the sun's path and yet
they're mortal men that fly over this ground before the sky
can shift, flesh and bone men that throw discus and javelin
so far, so fast they could make the winds lose their way.
As the day wanes there is jubilation and dejection,
unequally shared –
like divine favour, says a stiff-jointed loser
over a gifted jug of wine.

# Drunkard's Cloak

All my problems were brewed, bottom to top, in a barrel,
every ill fermenting further when taken without water:
from cask to cup, from cup to jowl till I was reeling ripe,
pickled, lushy, tipple-toxed and stiff, three sheets to the wind,
fuddled and stewed, I thumped the empty drum and met
the floor with a bow and the door with a shoe up my arse,
till nearly none a place would have me to fill their stools.
When a man's money stops being good enough to take,
that's when you've your head in the jakes, to be full as a goat
and still want more – I knew Trouble was my only friend,
forever casting up my accounts of the night before;
everyone else had left my house sure as time was called,
my next, and only, guests were the law.
Whoever said a judge is a sombre thing has not met those
that'll drop the drunkard's cloak around you;
I can hear his flesh-tub wibble with mirth as he does say
I must don a barrel about the streets, dry as dust, at that.
Though I may be spared spikes or whips or fines
I must take rotten apples aplenty to the head and remember,
the next day, how all the town saw me fall and roll and roll on.

# Prescription

You did not want proficiency;
you wanted certainty, the kind
that only comes via a promise or
a prayer.

You offered up your sacrifice;
coins soft and smooth as butter
and I, like a well-greased God,
pocketed them discreetly, blessing
your body with all that it is in me
to bless.

Quackery is such a sly, slippery word,
a mercurial spill of accusation – after all,
I gave you a fair return: a tea that could
as likely cure you as not, salts that will
revive you more assuredly than the close air
of your closeted home.

You may trust me as well as any man
with half a heart to preserve yours whole
in vinegar and a cloudy jar,
should you choose to give up
on these cures altogether.

# Power Sale

*I sell here, Sir, what all the world*
*desires to have – POWER.*
– Matthew Boulton

I have, here for you, a deep voice
that catches ears, a way with words,
a way of making them burrow like ticks,
ramrod posture, broad shoulders,
a stare more invasive than X-Ray,
an iron fist – please understand
the literal is never as impactful
as the imagined. A strong jaw,
that could masticate and spittoon
any contradiction. Stamina – sleep
is for the weak, power is an exercise
in strength, you must stretch and flex
every morning for that far-reach
and wide-range.

This service isn't just about what I can give.
Nature hamstrings Man. I filter, remove,
reshuffle the brain's frillier trifles;
no pesky empathy or sympathy,
the maths behind two sides
of an argument; superfluous,
there is only one: yours!
If you come away with anything
more or less than that conviction,
then, my son, you can have your
money back, with interest, minus time.

Let's move forward, tunnel vision
is included too, so there is no going back,
no second takes, no do-overs, no failure.
Sure, it slows you down for a while,
the weight of the crown, all the fawning,
lip service, begging, attempts to take you
down a peg or two
but momentum builds, unstoppable,
trajectory fixed –
soon you'll be flying, up, up, and off,
looming over everything, out of reach;
remember, horizons can't be impeached.

## *Bon Appétit* and breathe

I watch a lot of cooking shows,
I consider myself to be a morning person,
and I'm not so naïve that I don't see
the squeaky-new, pre-prepped stage-setting –
but every time I watch them whip up
fresh hollandaise for those perfect-pouched
poached eggs or briskly whisk pancake batter
then flip faultless fluffy discs layered with compote,
the wishful, hungry part of me spends
all her sense on a skillet and a half-dozen free-range eggs
and expects, at eight-thirty on a Saturday morning,
always after the longest week, to be *compos*
*mentis* enough to free avocado
from its casing without being gloved in green mush,
or to crack eggs without bits of shell sinking down
into the bubbling spit of translucent, yolk-huddled glaires
that frost over thick-white; a portal to delicious domesticity
closing, and there is always a hair, somewhere, in something,
toast pops too soon or burnt old-paper stiff and I must wilfully
forget the logistics of a Full English: sausages before bacon,
bacon before beans, beans before egg, because,
despite repetition,
there is always a mad rush at the end, when hobs
should have multiplied, unsoftened butter butchers
the toast and non-stick means nothing –
by the time it's ready to shuffle onto plates,
ingredients now indistinct, my aspirations have stewed,
coffee's cold, house full with fug of cooking fat
and I think tomorrow; tomorrow I will eat Coco Pops.

# In search of Heathcliff...

I learnt a few things:
ticks do not care if you are of a romantic
and highly strung disposition,
they will seek out your tender places.
Some at least are erogenous: knee-backs,
groin-fold and under-pit.

The sun will shine when you reach Top Withins,
though you wanted the long skirt in which
you trip-hiked across the moor to bluster
and snag upwards in the terse wind,
to be sodden-hemmed and your scarf-shawl
too thin to contain your shivers –
the day will be still, warm and dry,
families serenely picnicking.

When you are most immersed
in your day-dreams, seated on a rock
among the heather, mouthing Brontë's words –
and your own, you will be come upon
by someone you know – though not well enough
to explain your... strangeness.

When you stretch your legs up the hill at Haworth,
to seek well-earned solitude with Heathcliff
over coffee and thumb-brittled pages
you will see him
sharing every other table,
even with those
yet to break the spine.

# PART THREE

# Malady-Riddled

# I Was Mr Hoare's Pig-man, 1817

After the thinking-fool's Goose
and Marocco, Horse of Knowledge;
a primer for every cup-addled man
who's spent his money watering cobbles
and wants his fortune yesterday, there was Toby.
A more sapient pig, a more genial oracle,
a better-humoured almanac, there never was –
to the Public's eye,
but imagine this: you are manservant to a hog,
not his owner, mind, his lackey –
I had not the pennies to rub together
to magic a pig for my plate, let alone the stage.
'A Fine Figure of the Porcine Race'
and it was me that kept him that way:
rose-water-rinsed, almond-oil-rubbed
and face farded. Mr Hoare sold
my tooth powder recipe as his own;
cuttlefish and spirit of vitriol;
best knashed swine in England.
Listened while he laboured over letters
with Toby; I've never held any straight in my head
nor my hand. Perhaps the Public
would have been more astonished
to see me Spell, Read, or Cast Accounts?
I can discover a person's thoughts
without being prodded with a stick,
or other cheap tricks, but it was not my due
to promenade about Spring Gardens –
and Toby was learned, after all,
he knew my place was beneath him,
so I endured the head-butts, cloven-stomps,
bites and pointed squeals, I endured Mr Hoare's clouts
and talking-downs, missed suppers and forgotten wages;

but woes stack firmly, like bricks, and raised in my chest
was a wall taller than London's Tower,
so I snaffled handfuls of candied peel
and lured Toby to his rightful place.
I'm sure the Men About Town
gloated in cannibal-delight:
'How sweet to eat something so wise'.

# The Strangle-hold

*Upon the retirement of Britain's most prolific rat-catcher,*
*Mr Cassidy of Cassidy & Sons (1923).*

It's a swift curl about the rodent's neck
with a well-practised finger-flick,
follow on, one-two, with a thumb-jab,
at the base of the skull, just a small threp
where bone-ridge gives way to an empty pelt-pocket;
you'll hear a snap, quieter than a pulled wishbone,
then quick barrow-fling the limp bone-sack.
One time my fox terrier, a pup still, mistook my hand
for a rat; I gained a perfect appreciation of how her teeth
seek blood before the flaysome rattle
of her death-shake.

I smittle most by hand, dart an arm into the shadows;
same reflex needed to spear salmon.
I go wherever the job takes me, slip
like a wrist through a cuff at the railway arches,
eyes strengthened by the dark.
Let the tremble of trains up-quake a mischief
of furry bucks and does, pot-bellied dams waddle
along the ginnel-maze of tracks, fur oil-blathered
and thick, their kittens blindly scatter
at Gipsy's bark; I never include them in my count.

Point of honour that I don't block doors or gates
when I work in-house or garth;
if you're not quick be still –
that's why I'm retiring.
I have my own rooms to look to
and my own worn carcass to rest.

'Quick-Kill' Jack, the man that scholared me,
said the biggest test in last-years
is re-tuning the ears and dimming the corner of eyes
until you can't believe there ever was
such a pest alive.

# High Society, 1844

*A review the morning after
the Duke of Devonshire's party.*

It would be a rich bachelor
who thinks it's a good idea
to bring giraffes to the party.
After all, he is used to admiring
fashionable long limbs
in chic yet natural attire,
is at ease with their self-possession
and their height. Lofty chat
amongst themselves.
But what about us attendees
down here, the people who admire
sunsets and hot air balloons
with craned necks, who are a little
dowdy, though we've tried,
who don't enjoy the hunt
and are too self-conscious to graze,
for those of us who get by
seeming absorbed in others
and must now look about more often
to ensure we're not trampled on.

# Cataracts

*à la Jacques Daviel, 1747*

I have never been very good at pretty speeches,
too often fool-heart is prized over sense.
To say you are lost in someone's eyes – thought-frippery!
There is no shame in proclaiming the eye a shallow thing.
One quill-wit spun ophthalmology as crafty hours spent gazing
into fair optics, and I do, foul too but I never lose myself –
few can verse-horn a fat heel of romance
into the slim slipper of gain but I am not without sensibility,
I can appreciate cloudless sky, indigo and dark flecks of corbeau,
drake's neck and olive, drab and noisette, creamy whites
turning to piss with age, feathered with bolts of red vein.
I note it all carefully but nothing is as beautiful and cruel
as the opal cloud that obscures the lens; a hand
over a speaking mouth. Others can knock the light back in,
as though we are eggs to be cracked, my way
involves a knife in the eye.
I have never been very good at pretty speeches.

# Mary's creature

They are beautiful
because you can't see
how they were put together;
they talk of seeing cogs turn
when someone thinks –
they do love to tinker with an engine,
or eyes being a window to the soul,
though their definition of soul is unclear,
arousal felt when they see another's pulse
quicken under the skin –
these are exceptions to the rule.
They do not want to know
which key wound you,
they protest their mortality
too much,
their ignorance is beatific.
They can trace my making
like a draughtsman's plans
from scalpel-spliced crown
to cauterised toes –
acceptable on cold slabs,
toyed with by men
who would play at being God;
but Adam did not want
to know the world.
They are cast like him,
and I, I am the clumsy thing
that has cracked their mould.

# Waste: A History

We'll never really know what was crossed
with what, our best guess is *Dionaea muscipula,*
more commonly known as *Venus Flytrap,* turned
polytypic by splitting and re-seeding strands
of *Sundew* and *Bladderwort,* all of one genus,
more or less, quite natural, they surmised,
to combine them. Add a little bioengineering here,
a little bionic support there, resulting in
the volume capacity of a city rubbish truck.
All waste fed through jaws that looked no bigger
than the average man's head, but expandable
to the size of the, oft-cited, beach ball
(*circa 1991 A.D.*). Nature's safety-catch,
in the form of the two-stimuli trigger hair,
was considered unnecessary. It is fair to conclude,
without much specific citation, that this was
one of their primary errors in judgement.
They enhanced the plant's ability to form
a hermetic seal and digest whatever
it consumed, perfect to dispose
of all that waste, no need to reduce,
only to feed. Adapted it to self-propagate,
like garden-variety poppies, wherever refuse
was most pervasive, sowed a little AI
so the *Purgamentorum Comedenti* could
itself discern between refuse and other.
It did so with organic abandon.
Once the statistics became dire
*Homo Sapiens* had to disguise their true nature,
needed to cross-breed and reseed to escape
the crushing judgement of the *Waste Eater.*
Characteristically they could have chosen *Ivy* or
*Lesser Bindweed* but it would have been unscientific

to proceed on such a basis; they looked instead to the Ancients, remembered Daphne's escape from the cruel embrace of Apollo and took on the limbs of a *Laurel*. No name for this species survives. That too was an error in judgement.

# In Stereo

They say the best salesmen
are most easily sold to,
so, it's a compliment to say
that when they taught you to sell
you bought it whole-stock.
I remember those sun-bright
American voices booming
from the cassette player;
I didn't realise how much
motivation had pooled
and set in my psyche,
like grease poured
down the plug-hole, until
years later I flat-lined
at that interview
and cried angry tears on the bus.
Not because I wanted it;
because I couldn't make them
want me: 'always interview
the interviewer',
'never put off today...',
'make a "hmmm" into a hymn
praising you.'
I wasn't sorry when the tape snarled,
crimped and twisted no matter
how may times you twirled a pencil
in the spool. Before another arrived
preaching through the letter box,
I slotted radio-recorded mixes
into the stereo,
turning them up so loud
you were sure
they'd mush my brain.

# Town Hall Steps, Leeds

Current thinking tells us that all time
is happening all the time
and though I can't really get my head around
this idea, it does occur to me as I eat my sandwiches,
sitting on the Town Hall steps, busying a flake of old confetti
with my shoe, that if this current thinking is indeed true,
it means that while a couple kissed on these steps yesterday,
a man, right beneath their feet, added up the minutes
he would remain free. And it means that their marriage
could already have been as long as his life was short,
and that I was disappointed by my sandwich before the first bite,
and that this bit of confetti has always been stuck to my shoe;
evidence that thoughts move in circles,
reminds me days later of that man in his cell, that couple
out the door, and my place on the fringes of it all.

# Octopus Dreams

*octopus traps –*
*fleeting dreams under*
*summer's moon*
– David Barnhill, Bashō's haiku

Sleek jars dance their way beneath night water,
moving with the thickness of time passing in fever-dreams;
the octopus seeps in like a rapid change of sleep-scape.

My father says they are quite like us,
they too dream of a safe place to lay their heads.
We offer them refuge for the night

and then… he looks to his sticky takoyaki,
he masticates with the relish we reserve
for underscoring our barbarity;

the way teeth rip crispy skin from hot chicken
or gnaw pork gristle off the bone. Does the pot-octopus
have greedy dreams like this?

Dreams of layering minced crab and beak-worked whelk,
camouflaging tentacles amongst the coral,
siphoning a giddy expectation –

or are his dreams more expansive than mine?
Dreams of an unfound crevice shaped like a jar
where hungry men are as distant and unknown as stars.

# Salt-song

*for Kat*

Hold-fasts and sea-whips,
urchins and sponges,
sun coral and rock-weed –
their shy brine-glimmer
hosts a flash of dorsal and gill,
shimmer of scale and fin,
of fingers and breasts
and hair and skin.
I tell drowning men
that the song of my sisters
sinks no ships; they flounder,
disbelieving. I tell them
fool-hardy horizon-skimmers
blunt bows and split decks faster
than the sun sets; under they go,
life frayed as old rope.
What would we do with them all?
Can't beach them like whales,
can't set straight stern and sails
to send them on their way again,
can't fix their bodies that are
too much water already,
but we foam-flicker, skim their sinking
and linger like kelp, a last song
leaves our lips and fills their mouths,
they gulp euphoria, their boots
and bellies leaden with it,
till they are shored abed
as deep as the world goes.

# PART FOUR

# Settle & Soothe

# Pontefract Cake

I was suspicious that it didn't flower,
I'd heard that sun-bathed liquorice
bloomed silky blue purses that could
slip on the tips of your fingers like thimbles
but the roots run deep, so deep they needle
cellar floors and the ruins of buried walls.
My Pa's treat was always to shush us like pups
by giving us a stick of it to gnaw, but I better liked
the sweeter Pomfret cakes rattling in the jar
like new pennies being saved for a seaside day.
I like the inside of my mouth turned black
like a cavern and the echoes it sets off
down my throat, how it settles in the stomach
like a warmed blanket and fingers creep
to unscrew the lid for another.
I like to run my tongue over the rise and fall
of the stamped letters; a small miracle to read
with a sense beside your eyes.
Pa says this manufactured stuff will rot
the teeth right out of my head. He says
I'll be able to keep them in that jar I've emptied again.
I've looked up some strong words for my Pa,
not curses nor coarse stuff but book words
that sweet-savour almost as strong in my mouth;
I say Pa, it doesn't matter if its pressed and shaped,
I say, it's still medicine, *Glycyrrhiza glabra*, magic
words that sound like I've made them up, he has half
a mind, I can tell, to say so, instead he sticks his stump
of sweet wood, his Pontefract cane, back in his mouth
and chews. We savour quietly, each to their own.

# Bentley & Tempest Ltd.

Bodies hot and fibrous between hempen looms,
light falls in knotted cordage over spindleshanked
half-dayers scrabbling unchancy under and around
the snarl of work.

Skein of a tune is cat's cradled between long-shifters,
used to isolating thought from hand, until snary interruptions
gnarl half-heard song into machine-thrum.

The afternoon keeps its colour while one or two try to toit
what they've mundled; hours are knit into each yard and fold
along with scuff-dust and long hairs that grey and fall.

# Headingley's Zoological Gardens

It was a neighbourhood scheme
got up to filter the good air from the bad,
elevate the pursuit of leisure,
instil a Godly pastime
of servile abstinence, for a day a week,
while everyone, all things in common,
promenaded amongst the animals.

Time slips and there are walls,
or fragments of walls built into
the kind of homes I covet,
homes that, unless you note
the dates with care, seem older
than the botanical gardens,
seem too solid to have replaced
something that slipped so easily
from our imagination and then
slipped from sight –
left tantalising clues:
a bear pit
and Sparrow Park;
a neck-turn of land
on the corner of Chapel Lane
and Cardigan Road;
street names dissolve,
I am heady with the chitter
of house sparrows and zebra finches
flitting and frisking around an aviary
bigger than the terraced yards that cobbled
over those fashioned walkways and bandstand steps,
over those ha-ha tiers and ornate railings,
within a hair's breadth of that crenulated bear pit.

Time slips,
place slips to Rombergpark,
a living museum that smells
not of bones and thinning paper
but of spring, of blossoms still nesting
along the branches –
it is as vivid and as unseen
as the zoological gardens I miss.
I imagine your daydreams jostling for space
like cycads and palms in a hothouse,
I imagine your pen keeps moving
even though the light is so bright,
there on that seat by the bridge,
that it makes you squint.
Are you thinking
of Headingley's lost gardens?
Are you thinking
of Eden
and the inevitability of the history
I've dug up?
I feel as though I have misplaced those gardens,
that they must still be tucked away somewhere,
near the urban farm or the nature trail.
I feel as though they have slipped away,
they are water wearing away at stones
I believed were set and familiar,
I wish the gardens
would lay like a sheet of acetate
over the sketch of today.

# How to be a Hermit:

Prepare your thoughts.
Though your cell
should be sparse,
your mind should be
as filled with curios and keepsakes
as a Victorian drawing room.
Unbox them, carefully unwrap
and set them on the mantel
of your hippocampus;
do not take them for granted,
or let them gather dust
in the back of dim-lit corneas –
prepare a mind brimful
and contemplate.

# Second Date

*for Marcos*

I buy a full-skirted tutu, layered up like a black meringue,
three tabs of buttons from the odds drawer
and a length of ribbon, though I can't tell you just how long.

You tell me you have a market-bag of delights too.
We sit on the steps of the civic hall,
laying out deli-tubs of *taramasalata, tzatziki, hummus,*
faintly warm bread and olives.

You pronounce their names with a flair of authenticity
only slightly undermined by my having no measure of it.
I've never heard of most of these things;
a mallowy pink dip deceptive in its salty tang,
olives concealing stones.

Our greedy consumption; unaware of passers-by,
we played the buttons on a napkin-board of tic-tac-toe,
naively sketching out shared futures in the considerate
domesticity of packing up empty containers
and scrunched paper bags, neither noticing
our lunch hour had already passed.

# New house

Before our dust settled
and the house was slowly
unclenching its fist,
so that we could wake at 3am
and know, innately, we were home,
before we knew which way
to jigger the front door key
or how long it takes the oven
to flare the gas,
before we understood
the radiator whistles or
how the floorboards measure our feet
with a small see-saw of unsteadiness;
before then, while creaks bore the echo
of other footsteps padding
down the hall, the house gingerly
let us into its confidence
and gave up small intimacies
of the residents before:
a half-finished bottle
of nail-growth polish,
hair snagged in the plug,
doors marked with repetition
of fingertips, a muddy coat
under the stairs, offerings made
in tentative welcome,
while our safety pins and receipts
slip between skirting and cupboard –
our down-payment of losable things.

# Those hours

*for Finn*

They were hours that passed without moment,
without thought; deep sleep ferried me across
their dark expanse or else unease tingled
when I awoke during those witching hours,
hours I associated with dying or chronic unsleep.
Then you unboxed them: bright, full hours,
and the noises outside hinted that others knew –
those chittering birds had been keeping secrets;
the sky is never really lightless, the night
is never quiet – we sang and cradled while you fed
and teased us with drooping lids.
I missed the big canvas of sleep, I did,
but now when I wake in those hours,
wee hours that are yours, I wake differently,
ears pricked for all the sounds of you, then,
softly, I let in the night, let it sit peacefully,
leaning against me like a tired friend,
as I have always let those sun-full hours
pull me up and whirl again.

# Week 10

*for Mum*

Your dirty laugh fills the garden;
gleeful caw-caw, tavern wench, witchy cackle,
it escapes your mask, scatters newly-complacent birds.
We would not usually sit out on a day like this
but it is warm enough – we talk as though
the garden were all walls, trust ourselves to the air,
worry becomes miasma again,
dispelled over freshly-painted fences.
The corners of your eyes crease and crinkle;
memory fills in the rest, so that
scrolling through those photos
I'm surprised to see
only half your face.

# Once a year

smoked salmon framed by limp iceberg and squeezed lemon wedges, martini glasses smeared with neon-pink Rose-Marie, tomatoes cut *dents de loup*, doe-eyed Babycham and Snowball bottles litter the (extended) dining table, tangled in streamers and party popper innards, pulled crackers and torn paper crowns, hopped frogs, cast fortune fish and grease-soaked packs of mini playing cards, carcass of a bird-stuffed-inside-a-bird-stuffed-inside-a-bird, pulled wishbones and left-over nut roast, congealed sheen where roasties huddled in goose fat, gravy drips trip a path to a defrosted Black Forest Gateau, puddled in *kirsch*, chocolate wrappers lead, like Hansel and Gretel crumbs, from table to sofa, TV-light animates dozing, sherry-reddened faces, smooshed up under old blankets, new-socked feet nesting like mice.

# Reverse

Looking at things backwards is easier somehow,
following things from the start reminds you
of all the choices that had to be made:
roads undriven, and so the story pauses,
loses steam, while you wonder; wander,
down those 'what ifs', I guess it's just
taking the long way round; more life
for my money, if thoughts are still worth a penny,
if they're not taxed to the hilt or the hippocampus.
I am not the first person who has tried to work out
where to start, where to end – nothing is that neat.
Isn't it strange how neatness begins to matter?
Neat as ninepence, neat as a new pin,
but I prefer the unidiomised tidiness
of a folded blanket or a shirt;
memories matched cuff-to-cuff,
clear edges and lines safely stowed in drawers,
as if the mind is a muniment room filled
with labelled moments ready to file,
statements of regret pushed right to the back,
with all the other unsifted miscellany
my grandchildren can dispense with.

# Notes on the poems

*Sowing*

A florilegium is a collection of literary extracts or an anthology. The word is from the Latin *flos* (flower) and *legere* (to gather): a gathering of flowers.

- Bear's Eyes – a flower also known as Auricula.
- Merian and Marshal – Maria Sibylla Merian (1647–1717) a great artist-naturalist and Alexander Marshal (c.1620–1682) a gentleman gardener.

*Staying Under*

It was considered bad luck if a woman who had given birth left her house before she had been churched. There is a story, possibly apocryphal, of women who created hoods from the thatch of their homes in order to go out and about but still remain under their roofs, and therefore avoid bad luck.

*Visiting Mary Toft*

Inspired by Mary Toft (1701–1763) who convinced prestigious doctors she had given birth to rabbits.

*Wednesday's Child*

Reference to the nursery rhyme 'Monday's Child'. The line goes: 'Wednesday's child is full of woe'. The poem contains a number of references to superstitions surrounding changelings in folklore.

- Beldam – an old woman

- Mumping – to mumble, mutter.
- Caul-born – A baby born with a caul (piece of the amniotic sac) on its head was, historically, considered lucky.

*Widow Raleigh*

Written upon the discovery of a velvet bag that some historians believe was used by Elizabeth Throckmorton, wife of Sir Walter Raleigh, to carry his decapitated head after his execution in 1618.

*Bonesetter*

- Sally Mapp – also known as Sarah Mapp (1706–1737) was an English lay bonesetter. She was famous for performing astonishing bone-setting acts and for being a woman in a male-dominated profession. She started her own practice: 'Cracked Sally – the One and Only Bone Setter'.
- Bistoury – a surgical knife with a long, narrow, straight or curved blade.

*Muse, or that other thing...*

- Bathing at Gower Street – Reference to Elizabeth Siddal modelling for John Everett Millais' 1852 painting *Ophelia*. Elizabeth Siddal became ill after laying in the cold bath tub for hours at Gower Street while modelling for the painting. The poem also references the creativity of other female Pre-Raphaelite writers like Christina Rossetti and her poem 'Goblin Market'.
- Emily's Book – Reference to Emily Brontë and the belief of some that her sister Charlotte destroyed an unfinished manuscript upon her death. Charlotte also posthumously edited

Emily's poetry. The line 'strange and sombre powers' references a remark in a letter Charlotte wrote to their publisher criticizing Emily's writing in *Wuthering Heights*.

- Julian of Norwich – Julian of Norwich (1342–c.1416) was a medieval female mystic who wrote *The Revelations of Divine Love*, a text this poem references.

## We are Volcanoes

From a commencement speech by Ursula K. Le Guin, May 1986, Bryn Mawr College, Pennsylvania, USA: '*We are volcanoes. When we women offer our experience as our truth, as human truth, all the maps change. There are new mountains. That's what I want – to hear you erupting.*'

## Kneading

- Tuff – geological term denoting rock formed by consolidation of volcanic ash.
- Clastic – geological term denoting rocks composed of broken pieces of older rocks.

## Lilliput Lane

Reference to 'Lilliput Lane' collectable cottage ornaments.

- Top Withens – a ruined farmhouse near Haworth said to have inspired Emily Brontë when writing *Wuthering Heights*.

*Venus and Mercury*

Referencing the saying 'a night with Venus, a lifetime with Mercury';
mercury was used to treat syphilis. The poem lists archaic cures for
and symptoms of syphilis.


*Walter's Wife*

"Walter" is the nom de plume of a Victorian diarist whose memoir,
*My Secret Life*, detailed his sexual experiences.


*Miss An-nym—s, C-m S—n Lane, London.*

Written in response to *Harris's List of Covent Garden Ladies*, an eight-
eenth-century guide to prostitutes in London.


*Heart Stopping*

- angina – chest pain that occurs when the blood supply to the
  muscles of the heart is restricted.
- atrium – upper chamber through which blood enters the vent-
  ricles of the heart.
- pyrosis – heartburn
- rambles through Naples and France – reference to syphilis,
  which can lead to heart problems.
- carditis – inflammation of the heart.
- cardioptosis – downward displacement of the heart.
- aneurysm – enlargement of an artery caused by weakness in
  arterial wall. A ruptured aneurysm can be fatal.

*Seeking true ideograph*

- Ideograph – a graphic symbol that represents an idea or concept.
- Silphium – seeds believed to be inspiration for the shape we use to represent hearts.

*Drunkard's Cloak*

The drunkard's cloak was actually a barrel, with a hole at the top for the head to pass through. Two smaller holes in the sides were cut for the arms. Once the barrel was on, the wrong-doer was paraded through the town and pilloried.

*I Was Mr Hoare's Pig-man, 1817*

Inspired by illusionist Nicholas Hoare, trainer of 'Toby the sapient pig'. In 1817 an autobiography appeared called *The life and adventures of Toby, the sapient pig: with his opinions on men and manners. Written by himself.*

- Farded (archaic) – to paint the face with cosmetics/powder the face.

*The Strangle-hold*

- Threp – Yorkshire dialect for a blow or kick
- Smittle – Yorkshire dialect 'to catch'
- Garth – Yorkshire dialect for yard

*High Society, 1844*

The Duke of Devonshire threw a garden party at Chiswick House, London in 1844 to welcome the Russian Tsar, Nicholas I, and had four giraffes brought over from Surrey zoo to attend.

*Mary's creature*

A reference to Mary Shelley's *Frankenstein: or, The Modern Prometheus* (1818).

*Pontefract Cake*

A liquorice sweet made in the Yorkshire town of Pontefract. Also known as Pomfret cakes.

*Bentley & Tempest Ltd.*

Named after the Tempest family who ran Armley Mill, Leeds from the 1890s until 1969. Some archaic dialect words are used:

- Spindleshanked – Long, thin legs.
- Unchancy – Sometimes used to mean mischievous or unlucky, but also used to describe something potentially dangerous.
- Toit – From the phrase titty-toit: To spruce or tidy up.
- Mundle – As a verb, it means to do something clumsily, or to be hampered or interrupted while trying to work.

*Headingley's Zoological Gardens*

Written as part of a project celebrating the 50<sup>th</sup> anniversary of the twinning of the cities of Leeds and Dortmund, Germany. As part of the project I was paired with German writer Conny Franken to exchange writing and learn more about each other's and our own neighbourhoods. I discovered, as part of my research, that Headingley, a suburb of Leeds, once had a zoological and botanical garden, which opened in 1840.

- Rombergpark – a park in Dortmund, Germany.

*Once a year*

- Dents de loup (wolves' teeth) – a decorative cut used on food like tomatoes and lemon when served as garnish. Particularly evocative of '70s and '80s cuisine.

*Reverse*

- Muniment room – a storage room, often found in stately homes, for keeping family records.

# Acknowledgements

Versions of some of these poems have appeared in the following publications: *The North, Strix, Popshot, Brittle Star, The Valley Press Anthology of Yorkshire Poetry, Dear Damsels,* Mary Evans Picture House's 'Poems and Pictures' blog, *154* (Live Canon), *(More) Christmas Poems* (Live Canon), *The Fenland Reed, One Hand Clapping, Finished Creatures* and the Half Moon Books anthology *The View from Olympia: Poems Inspired by Olympic Sport.*

'Town Hall Steps', 'Leeds', 'Second date' and 'Bentley & Tempest Ltd.' were written as part of the Leads to Leeds project, during a poetry pairing with poet Tracey Martin. Many thanks to Helen Mort for my inclusion in the project. 'Headingley's Zoological Gardens' was written as the result of a pairing with writer Conny Franken, as part of the LD50 celebrations for the 50th anniversary of the twinning of the cities of Leeds, UK and Dortmund, Germany. Many thanks to Peter Spafford for my inclusion in the project. 'Staying Under' and 'Waste: A History' were longlisted for the Live Canon Poetry Competition in 2019 and 2020 respectively, and included in the competition anthologies.

Earlier versions of some of these poems also appeared on Twitter (@JoBrandonPoet) as part of my role as the 2018 Poet in Residence for the Bradford Literature Festival, who also commissioned 'Three Ages' as a poetic response to Gustav Klimt that year. I would like to offer great thanks to all at the Festival, especially Syima Aslam, Kelly Holt and Charlotte Broderick, who have been wonderful supporters of my work. I would also like to thank the Black Horse Poets in Wakefield for their editorial feedback.

Finally, I would like to thank Jamie McGarry for all his magic, Peter Barnfather for his design wizardry, my wonderful partner Marcos for his mischief and my beautiful son Finn for making every word sound special again.